This book is dedicated to my 3 little poopers.CG, GG, and EG. Mom loves you!

And to my best friend JG.

To my wonderful
family for always
believing in me.

SG

This awesome active baby gave his Mom and Dad joy.
But he's changing very quickly to an awesome little boy.

He wanted to poo where little boys poo...
in the potty!

Mom and Dad were very excited.
They took him to buy brand new underwear.

They taught him how the potty works.
And they got him a step stool to get up there.

It might take a while but don't get discouraged. Mom, said "Keep trying and you'll be encouraged!"

So they started their week with potty training on the mind.
How will it go? What will they find?

On the first day they went to the park. He was having so much fun and forgot to tell mom he needed to go. And so... he pooped in his pants.

Oops, babies poop in their pants. Little boys poop in the potty.

When you have to go, let someone know.

On the second day they were playing catch in the yard. He waited too long to get to the toilet. And so... he pooped in the grass.

Oops, dogs poop in the grass. Little boys poop in the potty.
When you're playing, take a break to see how your body is feeling.

On the third day they were playing fetch with doggy.

He went to look for the lost ball and realized it was time to go. And so... he pooped in the bushes.

Oops, caterpillars poop in the bushes.
Little boys poop in the potty.
Before you go outside to play, use
the potty at home.

On the fourth day he was playing with kitty.

He saw kitty go and wanted to know what it was like.

And so... he pooped in the box.

Oops, cats poop in the box. Little boys poop in the potty. The potty isn't scary, you will feel proud to use it.

On the fifth day they were playing at the pond. He wanted to swim like the little fishes.

And so... he pooped in the water.

Oops, fish poop in the water.
Little boys poop in the potty.
Going poop on the toilet can be fun.

You can sing a song when you're done.

On the sixth day it was raining, so they stayed inside to watch movies. And so... he pooped behind the couch.

On the seventh day he woke up and was ready to play. He remembered what mom said about going potty, and he knew exactly what to do!

He called for Mom and they rushed to the potty. Teddy came too so he wouldn't miss the occasion.

A few minutes went by, then.....

It finally happened. He pooped in the potty!!!

They used toilet paper to wipe.

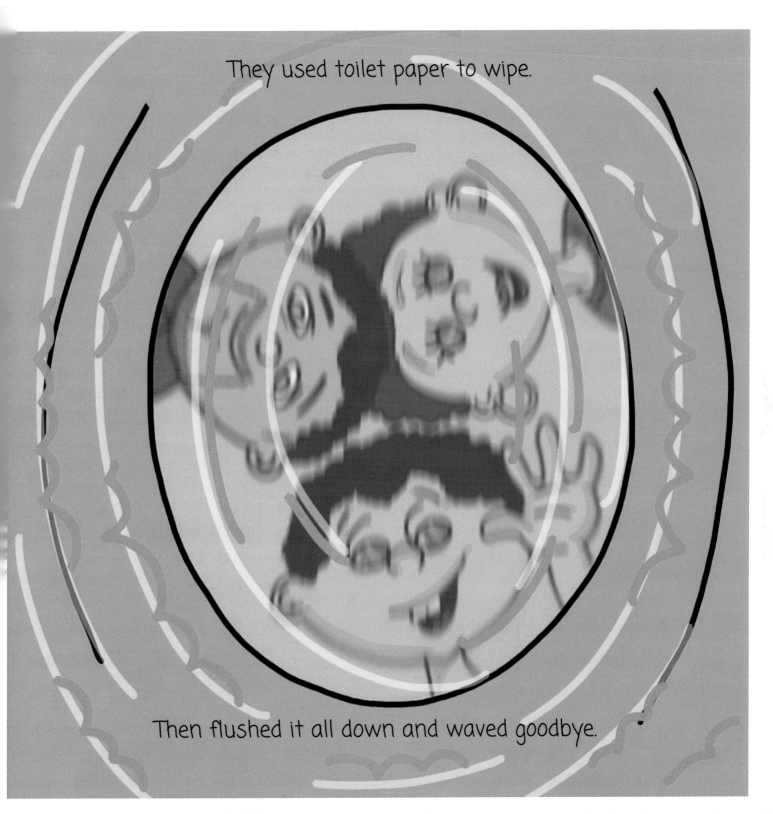

Then flushed it all down and waved goodbye.

He pulled up his pants
with a sense of pride.
And then he
washed his hands,
of course.

He called Grandma and Grandpa to share the news.
Then they celebrated with some cookies.

Mom and Dad smiled as their little boy grew.

Now he does what little boys do.

And now he poos where little boys poo....
in the potty!

The end....